CRINAN CANAL
The Shipping Short Cut
by
Guthrie Hutton

Two of these men opening the sea-lock gate at Ardrishaig are 'putting their backs into it', an expression thought to owe its origin to the practice of pushing backwards against the balance beam of a lock gate to open or close it.

Linnet descending the Dunardry flight.

© Guthrie Hutton 2003
First Published in the United Kingdom, 2003,
by Stenlake Publishing
Telephone/Fax: 01290 551122

ISBN 1 84033 257 3

ACKNOWLEDGEMENTS

I would like to thank Margaret Morris, George Waugh, Robert Grieves and Jean and Margaret Graham for letting me use some of their pictures. Their help allowed me to broaden the scope and content of the book for which I am most grateful.

SOME FURTHER READING

Cameron A.D., *Getting to know . . . The Crinan Canal*, 1978.
Duckworth, C.L.D., & Langmuir, G.E., *West Highland Steamers*, 3rd edition, 1967.
Hamilton, Forsyth, *Kipper House Tales*, 1986.
Lindsay, Jean, *The Canals of Scotland*, 1968.
MacBrayne, David, Ltd., *Summer Tours in the Western Highlands and Islands of Scotland*, 1912.
McDonald, Dan, *The Clyde Puffer*, 1976.
MacDougall, Lesley, *The Crinan Canal*.
Paterson, Len, *The Light in the Glens*, 1996.
Preston, Robert, *Days at the Coast*, 1994.
Ransom, P.J.G., *Scotland's Inland Waterways*, 1999.
West Highlands and Islands of Argyll Tourist Board Ltd., booklet No. 9: *Crinan, Lochgilphead & Knapdale*, 1992.

INTRODUCTION

The revenue cutter HMS *Daisy* in Ardrishaig basin.

Canal mania swept Britain in the second half of the eighteenth century and amongst the welter of ideas that were put forward at this time was one to bypass the hazardous passage round the Kintyre peninsula. It was promoted in Government circles as having the added benefit of encouraging development in the area and James Watt – better known for his work on steam engines – was commissioned to survey a route. He prepared a largely favourable report, but no public funds were made available to further the project and instead a private company, led by the Duke of Argyll, was formed to develop it. The company engaged the notable Scottish engineer John Rennie and, based on his detailed surveys, started construction in 1794.

The canal was short, only nine miles from sea-lock to sea-lock, but soon there was a lengthy list of troubles. The project was underfunded; landowners, including some of the company's own proprietors, insisted on high prices for their ground; and labour costs were also heavy. Navvies (the men who built canals, or navigations, were known as navigators or navvies) were unwilling to leave lucrative jobs on the many canal projects in England to work in this remote, wet corner of Scotland. The company had to resort to asking the army for help, and the Government for loans. Ground conditions made construction difficult and the elements conspired against the engineers, with storms destroying their work as they went along.

It was just one of those jobs where nothing seemed to go right, and when the canal was opened in 1801 it was in an unfinished state and because of concerns about the stability of the banks the water level was kept low to reduce pressure on them. Bad weather did cause an embankment to collapse in 1806 and water escaping from a burst reservoir dam wrecked part of the structure in 1811. These disasters drove the company deeper into a mire of debt and it again had to seek help from the Government. They were reluctant to bale out a private company with public funds and called in the great Scottish engineer Thomas Telford to evaluate the structure. He could have condemned it, but instead he proposed a range of improvements. These had been carried out by 1817, with the costs being borne by the Government, but the price the company had to pay was to relinquish control to the Caledonian Canal Commissioners. The canal had in effect been nationalised, but its future was secure.

Traffic on the Crinan Canal increased and in 1847 Queen Victoria passed through on her way to a holiday in the Highlands. She apparently found going up and then back down in the locks tedious, but her journey started a tourist revolution as tens of thousands of people followed in her footsteps, giving the canal a purpose it might otherwise not have had.

Passengers initially travelled on horse-hauled boats, but in the 1860s a little steamer called *Linnet* took over. Over time she became a familiar sight and also something of an icon for the canal. She shared the water with fishing boats and small coasters, but as their numbers began to dwindle, yachts and cruisers, manned by another kind of tourist, began to appear on the canal.

In the late nineteenth and early twentieth centuries plans were put forward to replace the canal with one designed for large ships, but these came to naught while small boats carried on using the old waterway. Now pleasure craft make up the bulk of traffic, and while the boaters use it as a superb short-cut between the Clyde and the West Coast, walkers, cyclists and horse riders have taken to the towpath to enjoy the spectacular scenery. So despite having had to surmount many odds, the Crinan Canal has survived to become one of the nation's treasures, a delightful, timeless asset in this mad, rushing, changing world.

Queen Victoria's trip through the canal may not have amused her, but it was a marketing man's dream come true. A succession of steamer operators – G. & J. Burns, David Hutcheson & Co., and David MacBrayne – milked it and other Highland trips made by the Queen and Prince Albert for all they were worth. By suggesting that their steamers were following in the royal wake, they promoted these services as 'The Royal Route'. It was not a single passage, but made via a series of steamers running between the Clyde and Inverness. The Crinan Canal formed a vital link in the chain, with the little steamer *Linnet* connecting with the sea-going paddlers at either end. She started operating in 1866, and is seen here at Crinan early in the twentieth century with passengers hurrying from the steamer pier to get on board and grab the best place from which to view the passage to Ardrishaig.

The Royal Route really got going under David Hutcheson & Co. They took over from G. & J. Burns in 1851 and through the 1860s began to expand their tourist routes. Pride of the fleet at this time was *Iona*, built in 1864. She worked between Corpach and Crinan until about 1886 when she was moved to the Ardrishaig run, to be subsequently replaced on the Crinan service by the steamer seen here, *Chevalier*. Built in 1866, she was smaller than *Iona*, but similar in appearance to her. *Chevalier* quickly became associated with the Crinan route, leaving Corpach in the morning and calling at Fort William, Ballachulish and Oban on her way south. At Crinan she met the *Linnet* and while the little canal boat scurried off to Ardrishaig, *Chevalier*'s crew brought out the paint and polish and gave their ship a daily makeover. She was, by all accounts, one of the best kept boats in the fleet; a shimmering, shining, spotless joy to behold. She, and the rest of the Hutcheson fleet, were taken over in 1879 by David MacBrayne, a name that, as a famous little rhyming couplet shows, became synonymous with West Highland travel: 'The Lord owns the world and all it contains, except the West Highlands, they belong to MacBraynes'.

Entertainment on the larger steamers would probably not amuse today's demanding public, but passengers then, on brief holidays from grimy industrial towns and cities, were transported into dreamland by the gentle homespun familiarity of it all. People 'wrapped up warm' to sit on deck, as these ladies in the 1920s have done on a steamer, thought to be *Iona*. Added to the bracing joys of taking the sea air was the music provided by small bands, or individual players like this man with his dulcimer. These musicians were not paid, but by 'passing round the hat' earned what they could from passengers' generosity. The other popular (male) activity was a visit to the engines – usually a thinly disguised excuse for a trip to the bar, although some men and boys actually did go to look at the polished, oiled magnificence of these machines.

Entertainment on a yacht was inevitably different to that on a steamer – there were, after all, no engines to look at – but periods of inactivity had to be filled somehow. On this boat bound for Crinan, the *Shira* of the Royal North of Ireland Yacht Club, the folk on board are engaged in a variety of activities. Reading and knitting are perhaps obvious forms of relaxation, but this yacht was also large enough to allow a version of deck quoits to be played, although a steady supply of rope quoits was probably required to replace those lost overboard. Yacht owners have long seen the value of the Crinan Canal as a link between the Clyde and the west coast of Scotland, so much so that the canal is now more closely associated with yachting and cruising than with commerce. It's not quite what the canal's early promoters had in mind, but it speaks volumes for their vision and enterprise.

Originally the canal was intended to encourage trade and also to bolster the local fishing industry by opening up more grounds to the boats and more markets for their catch. This certainly happened, and if this mid-twentieth century gathering of fishing boats in Crinan basin is anything to go by, appears to have continued after cargo vessels had become a rarity on the canal. Appearances, however, may be deceptive. When the canal opened, fish stocks were plentiful and something like 500 boats were chasing the famous Loch Fyne herring on both sides of the Kintyre peninsula. These plump fish were a household name in Scotland's towns and cities and, when sold as kippers from Ardrishaig's smokehouses, were highly sought-after. They became harder to get through the early years of the twentieth century as the industry struggled to cope with declining stocks, and by the late 1930s the fish had all but gone. The canal felt the pinch too as the number of boats using it dwindled. Some continued to work out of Crinan, although the once numerous herring shoals were no longer their principal quarry.

Crinan basin is less busy in this view looking past the post office and general store. The picture could have been taken any time between the 1930s and 1950s, although sometime close to the Second World War would seem about right. Regardless of the exact date, one 'sign of the times' is the notice advertising a single car for hire. Nowadays, at the height of the season, finding a place to park at Crinan can be tricky. Parking a boat can also be hard and many of today's boaters would think they had arrived at the wrong canal if they found the basin as empty as this. There is a buzz about Crinan these days with yachts and other pleasure craft cramming the basin. Some are just passing through on holiday, while others are there to take part in the annual races and rallies that attract numerous boats to Scotland's west coast.

Crinan basin is relatively quiet here too with only one yacht keeping a couple of puffers company. The picture was taken before a new sea-lock was built in the early 1930s to supersede the original one, which remained in existence as an extension to the basin. The puffer with the band around its funnel is sitting where the entrance to the new sea-lock was made. The banded funnel suggests it was one of Ross & Marshall's boats which had names ending in 'light', i.e. *Arclight*, *Polarlight*, *Raylight*, *Starlight* etc. The company ultimately became part of Glenlight Shipping Ltd. which continued to operate coastal shipping for the Highlands and Islands until 1993 when it was forced into liquidation by a subsidy regime that favoured road transport and ferries to cargo ships. Although it failed to arouse much public interest at the time, the loss of this industry was something of a scandal, but now, with concern for the environment growing, the argument for a revival of coastal shipping could grow too.

S.S. Pioneer at West Loch. Tarbert.

ARGYLL CANAL.

CAPITAL, £100,000, DIVIDED INTO 4,000 SHARES OF £25 EACH.—DEPOSIT, £2:10s. PER SHARE.

Provisional Committee.

His Grace the Duke of ARGYLL.

The Marquis of BREADALBANE.

W. F. CAMPBELL, Esq. of Islay.

The Hon. A. M'DONALD MORETON of Largie.

ARCHIBALD CAMPBELL, Esq. Yr. of Jura.

JOHN CAMPBELL, Esq. of Kilberry.

ALEX. M'NEIL, Esq. Yr. of Colonsay and Gigha.

ALEXANDER MORRISON, Esq. of Ballinakill.

WILLIAM DIXON, Esq. of Govanhill.

ALEXANDER DOWNIE, Esq. of Crossbasket.

ELIAS GIBB, Esq., Merchant, Glasgow.

DUGALD M'DOUGALL, Esq. of Gallanach.

JOHN CAMPBELL, Esq. Yr. of Islay.

With power to add to their Number.

It is proposed to construct a CANAL, navigable for Vessels of the largest class, from the Village of TARBERT, on LOCH FYNE, to communicate with WEST TARBERT LOCH, and thereby with the Atlantic. The Canal will be very short— only a mile and three quarters in length—and will save 140 miles of dangerous navigation to all sailing and steam vessels plying between the Clyde and the Caledonian Canal, the North and West of Scotland, and the Hebrides.

It will also very greatly shorten the voyage to all sailing and steam vessels between the Clyde and North and West of Ireland, and will prevent the necessity of their going round the Mull of Cantyre, one of the most dangerous and difficult head-lands to pass in the British Islands.

On looking at the annexed sketch, the immense value of this Canal to the Trade of the Clyde, to the West of Scotland, and to Ireland, will be seen at a glance. As a national object, no scheme has been proposed for many years more likely to be pro-ductive of general good.

To Parties wishing to invest their Capital, this scheme holds out prospects seldom brought before the public. The existing Trade of the Districts which will take advantage of the proposed Canal, will yield a large return, without estimating the increase that must take place in the present Traffic, or including Dues leviable from Vessels engaged in the Foreign Trade, although a very large Traffic may, with certainty, be calculated upon from this source. Numbers of vessels lie every year windbound, often for many weeks at a time, in the Harbours on both sides of the Mull of Cantyre, which need not be detained for a single hour after the Canal has been completed.

Applications for Shares to be made to

Messrs. J. R. DENNISTOUN & J. JARDINE, SHAREBROKERS, 53, RENFIELD STREET, GLASGOW; or to

ALEX. & JAMES MORRISON, WRITERS, 40, ST. VINCENT PLACE, GLASGOW, INTERIM SECRETARIES.

FORM OF APPLICATION FOR SHARES.

TO THE PROVISIONAL COMMITTEE OF THE ARGYLL CANAL.

GENTLEMEN,

I REQUEST that you will enrol my name as a Subscriber for Stock in the ARGYLL CANAL, to the extent of _____ Shares, of £25 each ; and I oblige myself, when required, to subscribe all the Contracts, or other deeds which may be thought necessary by you, and to pay the Sum of £2:10s. per Share of Deposit upon the amount of my Subscription, or upon any less number of Shares that may be allocated to me.

NAME _____

RESIDENCE _____

PROFESSION (if any) _____

REFERENCE _____

DATE _____

Glenlight's later coasters were powerful vessels, too big for the canal but strong enough to go around the Mull of Kintyre. The Mull, and the west side of the Kintyre peninsula, could be exposed to the full force of Atlantic weather, with strong tidal currents adding to navigational difficulties. The canal offered the only alternative to this hazardous passage for early sailing boats or small steamers. Passengers for Islay could avoid the Mull by disembarking at Tarbert on Loch Fyne and going over the narrow isthmus to join another steamer at West Loch Tarbert. The distance here from east to west coasts – a mere mile and three-quarters – encouraged a proposal in 1845 to cut a canal across it. This 'Argyll Canal' would have been significantly shorter than the Crinan Canal and offered savings on some journey times and passage fees. The plan was authorised by Act of Parliament in 1846, but investors were unconvinced and the idea fell. It was revived in the 1880s, but again failed to attract funds.

The yacht *Shira* has arrived at Crinan and come up to lie alongside *Linnet*'s wharf – her gangplank is lying beside the yacht. When the picture was taken the little steamer must have been bustling along the canal between here and Ardrishaig, or someone would have suggested to the crew that sail should rapidly give way to steam and to get their boat off the mooring. But, when the Good Lord made time he made plenty of it and clearly the *Shira*'s owners and crew were able to relax, take holiday snaps and enjoy their stay at Crinan. They are seemingly unmoved by the passage of a puffer which appears to be negotiating Lock 14 behind them – the mast and smoking funnel are visible above the lock edge. If the puffer was of no interest, the lock may have been; it was not constructed like the others, but instead was hewn out of solid rock and topped off with masonry. Also, it was bigger than the other inland locks so that large vessels could gain access to a dry dock that was proposed for the reach above it, but never built.

Shira is seen here heading east while the man and woman on deck appear to be preparing food – but what? They could have taken advantage of their stop beside a loch teeming with seafood to buy something exotic, or more mundanely – and more likely – they have stocked up on fresh vegetables and are shelling peas or beans. Regardless of what was going on in front of him, the smartly dressed helmsman – none of today's casual yachting garb for these folk – would have had to be vigilant for the next mile or so. This section of canal had to be hacked out of solid rock and is narrow with the offside punctuated by rock faces jutting into the channel. There are a few inlets where vessels can pass more easily, but for a wooden-hulled yacht going east, where the rule of the road required it to stay on the rocky side if it met a westbound boat, it could be a nervy experience. Perhaps that is why the woman is looking ahead so intently.

If there was one thing a yacht heading east out of Crinan would not want to meet, it would be the ungainly 100-plus tons of a laden puffer. These little cargo vessels, carrying supplies to Highland and Island communities, regularly used the canal. The *Anzac*, seen here heading west through Crinan Bridge, was owned by J. Hay & Sons Ltd. who operated a considerable fleet of what they called steam lighters. Most of their boats were built at Kirkintilloch on the Forth & Clyde Canal, but *Anzac* and her sister vessel *Lascar* were built by Scott & Co. of Bowling and launched in 1939. Their design was taken up by the Admiralty during World War II and used as the pattern for a large number of fleet tenders. These were known as Victualling Inshore Craft, or VICs, and although most were built in English yards, many were bought by Scottish coastal shipping companies after the war.

J. & J. Hay

106, MIDWHARF, PORT-DUNDAS,
AND
73 WEST NILE STREET,

AND AT DOCK PLACE,
GRANGEMOUTH.

Glasgow 11th Augt 1874

Mr Rhodis Esq   Dear Sir

We are in receipt of your favour of 10th inst with Table of Tolls for which we are Obliged

We are very much annoyed to learn that our Captain has not given in the proper weight, in most cases with the Coals the Steamer has to leave without B of Lading & this may account for any defficiency but the Mr Certainly ought to have gues[s]ed at something nearer the weight. We assure you it is quite Contrary to our wishes that any misstatements should be given in by our Captains

ought to know better as this Forth & Clyde Canal is wrought upon the very same principle. If you would kindly send us a statement of dues unpaid we will at once remitt you & will be glad to do so at any time. If our Men should come into your Canal at any time without Money — we trust you will see our wish to do what is fair with you & forego the penalty & we remain

Yours very truly
J. & J. Hay

Puffer skippers and their crews were known for being something of a law unto themselves. The exploits of these mischievous, carefree characters, whose lives were lived far from the strictures of a nine to five routine, were popularised by the tales of Para Handy and the *Vital Spark*. These stories by Neil Munro (written under his pen name Hugh Foulis) were made into a number of BBC Scotland television comedy series and formed the basis of the Ealing comedy film *The Maggie*, which featured a passage through the canal. That the character of the skipper Para Handy was based on some substance is borne out by this letter from J. & J. Hay to the Canal Engineer, William Rhodes. The sound of grinding teeth is almost audible as the exasperated company is forced to apologise for a skipper who has blatantly underestimated the weight of coal in his vessel in a failed attempt to pay a lesser fee for a passage through the canal.

The Canal Engineer was not just concerned with nuts and bolts: he ran the operation. He was like a colonial governor administering the affairs of a company based many miles away; on the canal, his word was law. He could be bad, or corrupt – or both, as some early engineers were – or he could be like William Rhodes: strong-minded, honest and incorruptible. As well as running the business, the engineer had to do what engineers do and look after the fabric of the waterway. One of the perennial structural problems was the Bellanoch embankment, seen here behind the *Linnet*. The engineers building the canal didn't excavate it here in the conventional way, but instead created this huge embankment along the shore. They used it to contain the water on the seaward side while allowing it to flood to a natural line on the landward side. The embankment was initially quite porous because the puddling (the process of sealing a canal with a clay lining) was poorly done, and a puddler had to be employed full-time to plug the leaks.

At Bellanoch itself the embankment spanned the mouth of a wide, natural bay which, when filled with canal water, formed a spacious lagoon. It was overlooked by these picturesque thatched cottages. They occupied an idyllic spot and were more modern than Hebridean 'black houses', boasting fireplaces and chimneys, but as time went on, and for whatever reason, people left them and they quickly fell into decay and ruin. The Bellanoch of today presents a stark contrast to this image of traditional West Highland life, and also to the time when the canal was busy with commercial craft. In those days, puffers and fishing boats rushed through as quickly as they could, leaving the lagoon unused. Now British Waterways has turned it into a busy, bustling yacht haven with rows of sleek, shining boats resting alongside floating pontoons – a scene that would have been unimaginable to the old cottage dwellers.

Bellanoch is situated on an extended crossroads. At the eastern edge of the lagoon, a fork from the canalside road heads south for Barnluasgan where it diverges, with one branch going to Tayvallich and the other to Loch Sween. Further east, at the main village of Bellanoch, the road to the north crosses the canal over Bellanoch Bridge. Thomas Telford was unimpressed with the original bridges when he surveyed the canal and these were mostly replaced by cast-iron swing bridges during the improvements completed in 1817. These appear to have been small versions of those on the Caledonian Canal, the only remaining one of which is Moy Bridge near Banavie. Canals like the Caledonian and Crinan, and the Forth & Clyde in the Scottish lowlands, shared a common problem: they were all used by masted sea-going craft which required clear air-draft (unrestricted headroom). All bridges therefore had to open and their design was constantly having to be refined and upgraded.

Opposite: As the volume and weight of traffic increased, the bridges had to be upgraded and the one at Bellanoch seen above was replaced with a swing bridge in 1892. It can be seen behind this fine-looking yacht. Beyond the canal the road crosses the mouth of the River Add on the Islandadd Bridge and heads, unusually for these parts, as straight as an arrow across the flat expanse of boggy meadow known as the Moinhe Mhor – the Great Moss. This unique area, rich in plant life and home to some rare insects and butterflies, was declared a National Nature Reserve in 1987. It would still have been flooded around AD 500 when the invading tribe of Scots came over from Ireland. After years of conflict they captured the Pictish fortress of Dunadd, situated on a rocky hill at the north-eastern edge of the moss. From there they set out to impose their rule and indeed their name on the country.

CRINAN CANAL · BELLANOCH.

HIRTA
SOUTHAMPTON

THE ENTRANCE HALL, POLTALLOCH HOUSE, KILMARTIN.   A.5614

Dunadd is to the right as the road heads north across the Moinhe Mhor; to the left is Duntrune Castle, a seventeenth century house within a stout defensive wall – a reminder of its a turbulent past. It was a Campbell stronghold until the Malcolms of Poltalloch bought it in 1792. Not content with the castle, they moved into a brand new neo-Jacobean mansion, New Poltalloch House (above), in 1849, but just over 100 years later, in the 1950s, they returned to live in the castle. To save tax, the roof was taken off Poltalloch House and it became a ruin, but far from fading away the name has become familiar to a much wider public because of the estate's gutsy little working dogs. Known as Poltalloch Terriers, they were deliberately bred with white hair to distinguish them from the wildlife they were flushing out of burrows and holes, and thus save them from being shot by mistake. They have become recognised in the dog world as the progenitors of those popular wee white bundles of unstoppable energy known as West Highland Terriers. Some early dogs are seen here at Duntrune Castle with estate gamekeeper William Young and two colleagues. William Young has his favourite dog, Boidheach Baan (Bonnie White [Boy?]) tucked under his arm.

HISTORIC CAIRN AT KILMARTIN.

Just north of the Poltalloch House parklands is Kilmartin Glen where one of Scotland's most remarkable clusters of archaeological sites can be seen. A Neolithic burial mound, used over a period of perhaps 1,000 years, is flanked by three later cairns from the Bronze Age. At Nether Largie and Temple Wood there are standing stones, stone circles and a timber circle, along with associated burial sites. Some of the stones have cup and ring markings carved on them, although the significance of these remarkable and occasionally complex designs is not known. The area has therefore been inhabited for at least 5,000 years, and the people have also invested it with a ceremonial or religious significance beyond mere occupancy. This has continued up to more recent times. The name Kilmartin – Martin's Cell – has early Christian associations and at St Michael's Church there is a collection of intricately carved medieval stones and this early Christian cross. The religious connection continues about a mile to the north where Carnasserie Castle, the home of Bishop John Carswell, stands beside the road. His 1567 translation of John Knox's *Book of Common Order* was the first book to be printed in Gaelic.

The Crinan Canal has fifteen locks with Nos. 1 and 15 being the Ardrishaig and Crinan sea-locks respectively. Lock 14 is also at Crinan and there are about three miles of lock-free water between it and Lock 13, the bottom lock of the Dunardry flight. Lock 13 can be seen in this view from Barnakill Farm which gives a good impression of the embankment that had to be built up to support the lock flight here – indeed part of the banking between Locks 11 and 12, to the left of here, failed in 1835 and the canal had to be closed while it was repaired. In front of the embankment is a track from the farm which goes across a bridge spanning Barnakill Burn; this takes off excess water from Loch a'Bharain, a canal reservoir. In the distance on the right is a small, thatched cottage (see inset), one of many – like those at Bellanoch – that survived into the twentieth century close to the canal.

The track from Barnakill, seen in the picture on the facing page, swings up past Locks 13 and 12 to this traversing bridge across the chamber of Lock 11. It is the only one of its kind on the canal and was installed in 1900 to replace the swing bridge which can be seen to the left of the *Linnet* on page 24. The operation of this swing bridge was a source of constant concern because sandy material underlying the chamber had caused the lock walls to settle unevenly. The problems were compounded by the use of locally quarried rubble stone in the construction, which was less robust than the coursed freestone of the Ardrishaig locks. The traversing bridge is operated by rotating the handle above the cogged wheel which makes the deck roll forward on rails to rest across the lock chamber. With the weight and movement of its mechanism set well back from the lock walls it succeeded where its predecessor had proved troublesome.

Linnet's decks are crowded with passengers as she heads west down the Dunardry flight, here emerging from Lock 11. The settlement problems at Lock 11 not only made its walls off-true, but meant that the chamber was smaller than the other inland locks. These were designed to be 96 feet long by 24 feet wide, with a rise of eight feet, although modern craft are limited by safety margins to a length of 88 feet and 20 feet beam. At 112 feet by 27 feet, the sea-locks were longer and wider than the inland locks so that the terminal basins could be used as harbours for larger vessels not going through the canal (Lock 14 was also larger – see page 12). The early puffers were made to fit through the smaller locks on the Forth & Clyde Canal, so they passed easily through the Crinan. Later vessels, which were built to meet the larger dimensions of the Crinan, were in effect made to fit the variations of Lock 11.

The five Dunardry locks, which take their name from a prominent hill to the south of the canal, herald a change of scenery. To the east the canal is enclosed by rocky tree-clad hills, but looking west across Crinan Loch the sights are spectacular. Closer to Crinan the vistas open out, and with the mountainous island of Jura in the distance these views from the Crinan's towpath must be unrivalled by any other canal in the British Isles. This picture looks west across the basin below Lock 9, with Lock 10 in the centre. The Add Estuary and Crinan Loch can be seen beyond the locks with the distinctive hill known as the Lion of Crinan in the distance. In the right foreground is the boathouse where *Linnet* was kept over the winter months. Here she was overhauled and spruced up ready for each new season.

On the south side of the canal, just to the east of Lock 9, was Daill, a hamlet of thatched cottages. It was in the news in October 1803 when the body of one its residents, Elizabeth MacKinnon, was found lying half naked beside the canal with her feet in the water. She had been strangled. Elizabeth had set out the previous evening to walk to Lochgilphead with her husband Duncan MacArthur, so he was the prime suspect. With strong circumstantial evidence against him he was tried at Inveraray, found guilty and sentenced to be hanged at the crime scene, beside the canal, on 31 October 1804. Before his execution he made a short speech accepting the justice of the sentence. After such an event, Daill was no doubt happy to sink back into obscurity and become a quaint distraction for the visitors who swarmed along the canal in later years. To well-to-do city folk, fed by the contemporary media on stories of empire and British supremacy, these houses must have seemed like the primitive dwellings of a 'native' tribe; objects to be gawped at for reasons unconnected with the dark and tragic past that lurked beneath their tranquillity.

There was another group of thatched cottages on the other side of the canal at Glac Connaidh. A short track led up to them from the towing path, which made them more accessible from the canal than those at Daill. Passengers from the *Linnet* often walked along this section of canal while the boat was working through the locks and so tourists, like the man in the late nineteenth century picture (left), could just wander up to them. He appears to have to have lain low for the picture, perhaps to avoid intruding on the 'natives', although the forebears of the wee girls in the upper picture were probably quite friendly. Dating from the early years of the twentieth century, this gives an interesting insight into contemporary mid-Argyll life. It was found with others which show that the occupants of the cottages grew vegetables, kept a milking cow and had horses, although it is not clear if these were used to help cultivate crops or just for transport.

Linnet is seen here leaving Lock 9 to go east along the summit reach; the towing path behind her looks like a causeway separating the main canal from Loch a'Bharain. The loch is a canal reservoir linked to the channel through a small bridge which can just be seen on the extreme right of the picture. The canal engineers knew that a summit of less than a mile in length would not hold a lot of water and so they made this loch, along with another smaller body of water on the south side, to ensure a head of water for the Dunardry and Cairnbaan locks. The summit is also fed from reservoirs in the Knapdale Hills, but these have often proved inadequate and, occasionally, unsound. Glen Clachaig reservoir burst in 1811 causing damage to Locks 5 and 6, and Camloch reservoir gave way in 1859 swamping over a mile of the a canal with water, mud and debris. Trees planted in the catchment area have also soaked up water and thus affected the supply to the reservoirs, and on top of this the canal has a bad history of leaking. In recent years, however, British Waterways has tackled the water supply problems, improving the reservoirs, patching up the leaks and introducing a system of back pumping from the River Add.

At the eastern end of the short summit pound is Lock 8 with Cairnbaan Store beside it. The store was a must on the itinerary for *Linnet*'s passengers because while she negotiated the locks they had time to get off, stretch their legs and inspect the wares. Also, *Linnet* was the only steamer in MacBraynes fleet which did not have a restaurant, so regardless of the direction people had come in, by the time they got to Lock 8 they were ready for some refreshment. The shop's interior was lined from floor to ceiling with richly coloured pine boarding, and the shelves were stacked with lemonade, chocolate, tobacco, postcards, souvenirs and all the other essentials a passing tourist might want or need. Outside, people could relax and enjoy their purchases, although the man in the foreground here has contrived to hide his personal weakness – munching chocolate perhaps, or smoking a fag – with his hand.

A funnel and mast are just visible here as the puffer they are attached to heads out of Lock 8. *Linnet* is approaching fast from the east and the puffer had better make its exit rapidly (which is probably a contradiction when talking about puffers) because the passenger vessel had priority over all other craft. Leaning on the balance beam to watch the proceedings are an elderly woman and a kilted man, either of whom could have inspired the comedian who invented the quasi-nautical expression 'avast behind'! (In the language of the sea 'avast' means to stop so the expression is both nonsense and very unkind, but if you get the point also quite funny.) The suitcase on the ground looks like a bagpipe case, which might suggest that the kilted man was a busker, there to entertain the passengers. Pipers apparently played for Queen Victoria at every lock as she passed through the canal, so our man could have been continuing a tradition started during the royal tour.

The coaster heading west down the Cairnbaan locks here is the *Anzac*, the same vessel that appears on page 14, but looking somewhat different. A stubby funnel has replaced her tall lum and the superstructure has been reshaped to provide better accommodation for the crew. This was done in 1959 when the vessel was converted to diesel. The introduction of diesel engines to drive coasters ended the use of steam power on the canal by commercial vessels. This had begun in 1819 when Henry Bell started a service between Glasgow and Fort William with the *Comet*. This boat, famous as the pioneer of regular steam services on the Clyde, was wrecked the following year, but the age of steam had arrived and soon many other paddle boats were using the canal. These in turn became either too big for the canal or were replaced by the screw propelled puffers. Steam puffers returned to the canal in the 1970s and 80s when restored boats *VIC 32* and *Auld Reekie* began to ply their trade as holiday craft. Steam enthusiasts among the passengers could enjoy a sweaty trip into fantasy-land by stoking the boiler.

Queen Victoria's holiday in the West Highlands in August 1847 caused great excitement, and nowhere more so than in mid-Argyll when it became known that she intended to sail along the Crinan Canal. A floral arch bearing the words 'Queen of Highland Hearts, Welcome' greeted her at Ardrishaig and the pier was laid with a tartan cloth – the local equivalent of a red carpet. A carriage took her through the village to the barge *Sunbeam*, which had been specially fitted out and brought to the canal for the occasion. Two postillions, dressed in royal livery, rode the towing horses which took the boat along at a brisk pace. Prior to the event, commentators expressed surprise that in this age of steam the Queen should be subjected to such a slow, antiquated method of transport. She may indeed have found it tedious, but she was also observed taking an interest in aspects of the canal's operation and pointing these out to Prince Albert. She certainly thanked those responsible for her safe passage which concluded just after 7.00 p.m., about two hours after her arrival at Ardrishaig. At Crinan she boarded the Royal Yacht *Victoria and Albert* which had sailed round Kintyre. While she dined, the people of Ardrishaig and Lochgilphead lit bonfires and celebrated.

The only craft operating internally on the canal were the passenger boats – all other vessels using the waterway were sea-going. In the pre-steam days, this meant sailing vessels and when these came into the canal they had to be tracked, or towed, by horses. The people who built the canal clearly expected the volume of traffic to be heavy because they built it with a towing path on each side between Ardrishaig and Crinan Bridge. Most other canals had a path on one side only and a standard procedure was followed which allowed boats to pass without having to let go of their tow lines. On the Crinan, as steam or diesel engines became the norm, the use of horses diminished. However, as this picture of the *Shira* at Cairnbaan shows, some yachts still needed help and tracking with a horse continued for unpowered craft until 1959.

The name Cairnbaan – it means White Cairn – is yet another indicator of the richness of the archaeological heritage in this area. The Bronze Age cairn is to the south-east of Lock 5, behind the spot from where this picture was taken. There are cup-and-ring marked stones to the north of Lock 5, and at Achnabreck, beside the old Lochgilphead road, a rock known as the 'Stone of the Hosting' is covered in such carvings. Flint workings at Badden; a single standing stone (the 'Stane Alane'); and habitation sites around the head of Loch Gilp all add to the rich pre-history of the area. This view, dating from the more recent late nineteenth century, shows *Linnet* entering Lock 5, the bottom lock of the Cairnbaan flight. Between here and Lock 4 at Ardrishaig is the longest pound on the canal. It is about four miles long and 32 feet above sea level. In the background is the Cairnbaan Hotel which was built about 1800 to cater for canal travellers. It was, at one time, a temperance establishment, a situation today's drouthy boaters would regard as tantamount to cruelty.

The proprietors of the hotel, and those of Cairnbaan Store, were not the only ones intent on relieving the tourists of their disposable income. Lock-keepers, their wives and other local people used to set up tables at vantage points during the season to sell lemonade, milk and home produce. Here, in a picture which has unfortunately been blurred by camera shake, one such table can be seen in the background, with a woman beside it. The picture was taken from behind the wall in front of the Cairnbaan Hotel. It also shows a sign advising passengers what to do and where to go to change their means of transport. Cairnbaan was at a road junction and people could transfer here from the steamer to charabancs or carriages which took them on to other destinations.

There is something odd about this picture looking west toward Cairnbaan. It appears as if someone has missed the boat, forgotten to get off, or left something behind, but whatever has happened it is a curiosity. The vessel is the *Conway*, the canal's ice-breaker, which was used in the summer season to take those passengers which *Linnet* could not accommodate. She would normally therefore be sailing from one end of the canal to the other, so why she has put her nose into the bank at this point is a mystery. Apart from the reasons already guessed at she may on this occasion have only been taking passengers from Ardrishaig to meet coaches at Cairnbaan, and may be turning before heading back. Another vessel used to provide overflow cover for *Linnet* was the *Comet*, a boat whose name echoed that used by Henry Bell for his pioneering steam vessel. This new *Comet* was also a pioneer – she was MacBraynes first motor vessel, joining the fleet in 1907. She was not based on the canal, only coming in when needed, and was not the prettiest of boats, which no doubt explains why pictures of her on the canal are as rare as hens' teeth. Pictures of *Conway* are also rare, but by contrast *Linnet* must be the most photographed canal boat in the country – maybe even the world!

The canal's operators have always tried to take small boats through in groups so that they can be put into locks together, thus saving effort and – more importantly – water. These yachts working through the canal in 1902 have also found the practice to their benefit, because the horse in the distance, being ridden by the tracker, is towing at least three boats and the owners will no doubt have shared the fee. The picture appears to have been taken on the pound between Cairnbaan and Lochgilphead across Oakfield Moss. Canal builders were perhaps the first civil engineers to face the problem of constructing transport routes across bog land, but where the Forth & Clyde's engineers triumphed at Dullatur, those on the Crinan came unstuck at Oakfield. The embankment across the bog sank into it and had to be raised, and then the whole thing was washed away in a flood in 1805. The canal was closed for a year while it was remade on a new line, a wide sweeping bend hugging the firm high ground to the south.

Oakfield Bridge, a swing bridge made at P. & W. MacLellan's Clutha Ironworks in Glasgow in 1871, allowed local light traffic to cross the canal. Seen here with *Linnet* heading west, it was the nearest point to Lochgilphead that boats of any size could reach because the loch's shallow, shelving beach would have made any pier impossibly long. Because it was on the canal, the wharf beside the bridge had the added benefit of being non-tidal, which meant that coasters like the one on the right here could come alongside at any time to deliver supplies. There was also a coal yard – or 'ree' to use the Scots' word – beside the bridge. The coal was delivered by puffers coming across from Ayrshire or the Clyde and distributed throughout the area on carts. The ree was run by the bridge-keepers, one of whom, William Miller, was there for so long that the bridge became unofficially known as Miller's Bridge.

Miller's Bridge is just out of the picture on the right of this view looking across the canal to the bridge-keeper's cottage. The house is contemporary with the canal, having been erected about 1800, although the section with the sloping roof on the left-hand side, and the lean-to at the front, are later extensions. At the back, facing the road, are two windows and an arched entrance to a basement store. This is below towpath level and makes the building look like a much larger structure when viewed from the road than the cottage-like appearance suggested by the facade fronting the canal. Sitting alongside the wharf is a Tarbert registered fishing boat. Fishing boat numbers usually – but not always – start with the first and last letters of the port of registry, which for local boats in the early 1950s, when this picture was taken, meant the TT of Tarbert. Prior to 1907 Loch Fyne boats were registered in Ardrishaig and sported the letters AG along with their number.

There is an almost Wild West feel about this picture of Lochgilphead's Argyll Street with two men riding into the deserted town. In these days of the omnipresent motor car it is hard to imagine the town looking so quiet, but perhaps the picture was taken on a 'flag day', a day when a charity collection was taking place. There used to be fewer of these, and before the advent of easy-peel stickers, donors would be given a little flag on a pin – hence the term. Old-time comedians could always rely on getting a laugh by alluding to deserted streets in Aberdeen as typical of the city on a flag day and a reflection of it's meanness – but Lochgilphead? Perhaps the people have all stayed away to avoid the pre-motor car form of pollution which horses have left scattered liberally on the road. In the background is the Parish Church, which was erected in 1885 to the designs of Glasgow architect John Honeyman.

The canal changes its scenic face yet again as it runs along the side of Loch Gilp. The hills seem gentler, the trees regenerate naturally and Lochgilphead forms a different kind of backdrop – one with buildings and beaches. It can be seen in the background of this (frustratingly fuzzy) picture of *Linnet* heading for the west coast. She is accompanied by a number of people on the towing path who seem to be having little difficulty keeping up, despite those long Edwardian dresses. It is also possible to follow the canal on the south side here because the path-cum-road, known as the 'back bank', has been kept in good order by continuous use between Miller's Bridge and Ardrishaig. It is not recommended for those of a nervous disposition, however, because halfway along is the site of the old Kilduskland Chapel where walkers have encountered a feeling of cold expectancy before seeing ghostly figures.

Linnet originally operated at Ardrishaig from a berth between Locks 3 and 4, but this was later changed to one just above Lock 4. This move was presumably made to save time and, possibly, water. The lower pound was wide, allowing plenty of space to turn the boat, whereas above Lock 4 the width was restricted as seen here with *Linnet* turning before coming alongside. To turn a boat in the confined waters of a canal the bow is carefully run against the bank and, with the engine driving forward, the helm is put hard over. This keeps the bow more or less stationary while the stern swings around until the boat reaches a point where it can be reversed off, facing in the opposite direction. The manoeuvre, called 'winding' – with the first syllable pronounced as in gale force wind – is one of many words and phrases spawned by canals. Some of these have been absorbed into everyday use, while others remain peculiar to the private and timeless world of canals.

Linnet is seen here at her original berth just above Lock 3. Compared to the elegant paddle steamers that she operated in conjunction with, she was an odd-looking little boat, but was well suited to the job she performed. Her finely shaped hull cut through the water with a minimum of wash, although it was somewhat hidden beneath the white-painted, high-sided superstructure. Her red and black funnel was made deliberately tall to throw the copious amounts smoke away from the decks. The engines exhausted up the lum to provide the draft for the furnaces and drove twin screws making her a powerful and highly manoeuvrable vessel. She operated during the four summer months only, completing the return run between Crinan and Ardrishaig every day. Her last season was in 1929 after which she was sold to a motor boat club which based her on the Gareloch as clubhouse. Sadly, away from her natural environment, her high-sided superstructure was vulnerable to strong winds and she was wrecked in a storm in 1932.

Describing anything associated with the canal at Ardrishaig can be tricky because here it runs almost due north/south while actually going between the east and west coasts. Munro's boatyard, for example, was on the west, or south bank between locks 3 and 4. They built some fine fishing boats at the yard like the one seen sitting alongside here. Loch Fyne men were known throughout the fishing world for their skilled handling under sail of these small, open-decked craft. Behind the boatyard is the large and imposing Rockhill House which was erected in the 1890s, about the time this picture was taken. It was one of many fine villas looking out across the canal and Loch Gilp to the east – or should that be north?

The boatyard and smithy can be seen here beyond the lock, while just visible at the right-hand edge of the picture are the 'stances', wooden frames where fishermen dried their nets. Dominating the view however is the short, slightly dog-legged pound between Locks 2 and 3 where boats rarely, if ever, tied up because of the high sides and steeply shelving banks. As a result the pound looks empty and therefore somewhat different to the rest of the canal at Ardrishaig, but this lack of activity on the water is not matched by the tracking path which is busy with sheep being herded into town. Ardrishaig folk were used to seeing animals like these being driven to the pier where they were put on steamers and taken to market in Scotland's central belt. Cattle were also driven into town and sometimes made quite a spectacle when going across the canal bridge. The bridge, with its open railings, tended to frighten the animals which could baulk at it; a few caused mayhem by turning back while others tried to run around it and went into the canal. The problem was solved in the 1930s when the present high-sided swing bridge was installed.

An unladen puffer could look very large indeed as this picture of *Glenrosa* entering Lock 2 shows. *Glenrosa* was a VIC boat bought by G. & G. Hamilton of Brodick after the war and was a regular user of the canal. Hamilton's amalgamated with another operator, C. McPhail, in 1948 and the combined company, Hamilton & McPhail, joined forces with J. & J. Hay of Kirkintilloch in 1963 to form Hay–Hamilton. They in turn amalgamated with Ross & Marshall to become Glenlight Shipping Ltd. in 1968, the 'light' part of the name being taken from the names of Ross & Marshall's boats and 'Glen' from Hay–Hamilton's. There appears to be an old upright boiler – the kind commonly used in steam lighters – sitting on the lockside behind the open gate on the right. In the background, visible between the old boiler and the boat, is Ardrishaig's war memorial.

The steam lighter waiting to leave the canal here is also a former VIC boat. She could be the *Glenrosa*, although frustratingly shadow has obscured her name. She is sitting in the entrance to the sea-lock with the swing bridge barring her way. The bridge was installed about 1932 to replace the old swing bridge at a time when the canal was being upgraded and repaired. As part of those improvements a new sea-lock was built at Ardrishaig. It superseded the original lock and projected beyond it by about a lock's length to create space for the new bridge. The old lock can be seen to the left of the puffer, with a fishing boat sitting in it. There were plans to use it as a dry dock, but these were never carried out and it simply became a handy extension to the basin. Ardrishaig was selected as the site for the eastern sea-lock because the water here was of sufficient depth for vessels entering or leaving the canal, even though this meant cutting the channel for some distance along the Loch Gilp shoreline.

A puffer can be seen here heading out of the old sea-lock past the breakwater. This was built to protect vessels using the sea-lock, but it proved too short to begin with and was progressively extended to provide greater shelter. Large numbers of small fishing boats congregated in its lee and some vessels also used the breakwater as a pier, although its shelving construction made it unsuitable for this purpose. As a result, a proper pier was built and this was also progressively extended as boats increased in size. This picture was taken from the pier, and as well as the departing puffer it shows a small fishing boat sitting on the hard standing above the slipway. The making of the canal, with its substantial breakwater, created a harbour at Ardrishaig for the first time. Fishing families came across from Ayrshire to set up a new fishing fleet and start a new life. It was a tough, precarious existence, and these fisher folk had to struggle by with little housing and no real community to shelter them. But they prevailed, and along with the people who came to work on the canal, established what was in effect a new town. The canal and its spin-offs have therefore combined to make Ardrishaig a somewhat unusual Highland town, with many of its people of lowland origin.